COOKING
FISH AND GAME

COOKING FISH AND GAME

French-Canadian Style

Francine Dufresne

101 Productions, San Francisco
1975

Illustrations from the archives of
California Academy of Sciences
San Francisco Public Library

Printed and bound in the United States of America

In the United States published by 101 Productions
834 Mission Street, San Francisco, California 94103

Distributed to the Book Trade in the United States
by Charles Scribner's Sons, New York

In Canada published and distributed
by Van Nostrand Reinhold Ltd., Toronto
ISBN: CANADIAN EDITION
paper 0 442 29925 7   cloth 0 442 29924 9

Originally published as *Cuisiner Poisson et Gibier: Un Jeu d'Enfant*
by Les Éditions Dufresne et Richard Inc., St-Léonard, Québec.
Translated by Jacqueline Stratford

Library of Congress Cataloging in Publication Data

Dufresne, Francine.
    Cooking fish and game, French Canadian style.

    Translation of Cuisiner Poisson et gibier.
    Includes index.
    1. Cookery (Fish)   2. Cookery (Game)   I. Title.
TX747.D8313   641.6'9'09714   75-25760
ISBN 0-912238-75-5
ISBN 0-912238-69-0 pbk.

CONTENTS

THE PLEASURES OF

To bag one's own moose is marvelous. To relish and savor it at the family table is the crowning experience. To weave along the banks of Québec's Matane River in search of the finest salmon of the year, to be out on the first day of the duck-shooting season at Montmagny or Lac Saint-Pierre, at Beauharnois or James Bay, to tramp happily through acres of muddy marsh and fields of reeds, to know the exhilaration of waking at dawn and taking the first duck of the season—all these experiences represent as many pleasures and thrills as they do memories. But to see the object of these delights and of so many arduous hours spent hunting in the wind and rain or fishing in the half-light of early morning—to see this precious prize get nothing but a third-class funeral in your neighbor's garbage can, or in your own, on the pretext that one has never cooked fish or game, is decidedly a misfortune. Worse—it's a real catastrophe. Many husbands have to beg and badger before their wives will finally consent to prepare one humble teal for them. This is really the height of foolishness and ignorance on a continent as rich in game as ours.

I take great pleasure in hunting wild duck and geese, in stalking deer, in peppering a flustered partridge, in teasing a speckled trout or salmon, or in annoying some wily old black bass who has certainly seen plenty like me before. But I take just as much pleasure in transforming these things into succulent and memorable dishes that will make the fussiest old gourmet's mouth water. Succulent and memorable yes, but also dishes that have nothing miraculous or magic about them.

FISH AND GAME

If you want to be a good cook, experiment—experiment and don't take yourself too seriously. If a recipe says, "slice the onions," and you feel like chopping, go ahead and chop. Experiment and use your imagination with herbs and spices too. The combinations and proportions I've used in my recipes are merely suggestions: I would probably never make a dish the same way twice. If you're in love with tarragon, add more. If you don't like sage, leave it out. And remember, herbs don't bite. Don't be afraid of them. I'm always surprised to see people looking at herbs as if they are a mystery. Herbs are delicate and gentle; they just want to help you.

Every good cook should have pots of fresh herbs on the kitchen windowsill, especially parsley, garlic and chives. I love sometimes to use a lot of garlic in my recipes and it is essential to have a garlic press to squeeze out the complete essence from the cloves. (If you like garlic as much as I do and don't want your boyfriend to know you have been eating it, eat a bouquet of fresh parsley afterwards. Parsley kills the smell of the garlic, and it's good for you too.)

For someone who really likes to cook, an interesting way to proceed is to sit in your living room and imagine the taste of various herbs and spices. People should dream of what they want to eat before they start cooking, because cooking should be fun, simple and at the same time an exploration. If it isn't, you may as well buy a TV dinner.

Francine Dufresne

FISH

Cooking fish requires a little care and attention because it is fairly easy to overcook. In general, all fish is done if it flakes easily when a fork is inserted in the flesh and lifted slightly, and if the flesh is no longer transparent. When cooking fish with white flesh, always sprinkle it first with lemon juice to preserve the whiteness.

You will find suggestions for cleaning, scaling and filleting fish on page 137.

FISH POACHED IN THE OVEN

Fish fillets are particularly suitable for this method of cooking. Place the fillets in a well-buttered pan and cover them with 1/2 cup of milk, cream or white wine, according to your taste. Then sprinkle with salt and pepper and a touch of nutmeg or paprika and add a few small lumps of butter on top. Bake in a 350° oven until the fish is no longer transparent and flakes easily.

FISH FRIED IN DEEP FAT

There are three basic ways to prepare fish for frying:

- Dip it in well-beaten eggs and then in fine bread crumbs.
- Let it soak in milk and then roll it in flour.
- Coat it with a commercial batter.

The fryer or saucepan should be heavy and contain enough oil or fat to cover the fish completely. It is best to only cook a small quantity of fish at a time. The oil or fat should be very hot in order to give the fish a crusty exterior which protects the flesh and helps it to retain its natural flavor.

This is my version of the classic base for fish cookery.

1 carrot   4 cups water
1 onion   salt and pepper
1 garlic clove   1 cup dry white wine
2 celery stalks

Cut up the vegetables, combine with all other ingredients in a saucepan and simmer for 1-1/2 hours. To cook fish in court bouillon it should preferably be wrapped in cheesecloth and the heat should be kept very low. Fish should never cook too quickly, because the slower it cooks the better the taste. You should allow about 10 minutes per pound when using this method.

On days when I'm feeling a bit limp and haven't the slightest inclination to cook, much less to perform feats of daring and imagination in preparing a fish, I take out my good old all-purpose recipe called The Lazy Cook's Way Out. The result is always very good.

1 whole fish, any kind
2 tablespoons olive oil
finely grated rind of 1 lemon
3 or 4 bay leaves
1 to 2 cups beef consommé

butter
few grains cayenne pepper or
  pinch paprika
2 or 3 slices bacon (optional)

Coat the fish on both sides with the olive oil. Put the oiled fish in a baking dish and add the lemon rind, bay leaves and enough beef consommé to maintain the moistness of the flesh. Top with a few dabs of butter and cayenne pepper for pep or paprika for color. If you are feeling a bit more perky, add 2 or 3 slices of bacon. Bake in a 350° oven allowing 10 minutes per pound.

For the stuffing and garnishing of a 4- to 5-pound fish.

1 pound butter
4 garlic cloves, finely crushed
finely grated rind of 1 lemon
1 teaspoon minced parsley

1 teaspoon minced tarragon
pinch each thyme and cayenne pepper
salt and pepper

Let the butter reach room temperature so that you can work it easily. Add the remaining ingredients and mix well. This is delicious simply melted in a saucepan over very low heat and served with a boiled fish or with one cooked on a spit, or as a stuffing for fish baked in aluminum foil. Spread the butter on the inside and outside of the fish, wrap in foil and bake at 350° for 10 minutes per pound.

For a light Friday night supper when you're tired.

1 cup cooked leftover whitefish	2 tablespoons butter
2 potatoes	salt and pepper
1 cup milk	

Cook the potatoes in salted water until they are good and tender. Drain and cut into small cubes and put in a saucepan with the milk and the fish and cook several minutes. Add the butter and seasoning and serve.
Serves 2.

Don't forget that garlic is good for people who have problems with the heart and circulation, and that it is said to promote clarity of mind.

1 bass (2 to 3 pounds)	1 pound fresh mushrooms, sliced
1/4 to 1/2 cup olive oil	butter
salt and pepper	1/2 cup tomato paste
5 or 6 garlic cloves	

Remove the bones from the bass; then wash and dry the fish inside and out and coat its sides with olive oil. Place the bass in an ovenproof dish and sprinkle with salt and pepper. Surround it with the garlic. Bake at 325° allowing 35 minutes to the pound. While the fish is cooking, fry the mushrooms in butter and when they are done, add the tomato paste. Pour this mixture over the bass before serving.
Serves 4.

Jean René is my favorite nephew and my spiritual son. This recipe is named for him because the taste of it is as much a pleasure as is his smile for me.

4 large fillets of black bass (about
   2 pounds)
4 large potatoes, peeled and thinly sliced
2 large onions, thinly sliced

salt and pepper
butter
2 cups milk

Wash, peel and slice the potatoes and onions. Line the bottom of a glass baking dish with a layer of potatoes, then a layer of onions. Add salt and pepper and a few lumps of butter. Lay the fish on top of this, then cover it with another layer of potatoes and another of onions. Sprinkle again with salt and pepper, dot with butter then pour the milk over top to cover. Bake at 375° for 1-1/2 hours.
Serves 4.

Marie Mignonne is my sister-in-law. She is the type of sister-in-law any woman who has problems of competition with other women should have, because she knows how to put herself in a "let-it-be" situation.

1 2-pound pike
2 tablespoons butter
1 medium-size onion, minced
1 garlic clove, crushed
1/2 pound fresh asparagus, chopped

1/4 cup milk
salt and pepper
chopped parsley
grated Parmesan cheese

Melt butter and sauté onion in it until golden. Add garlic and asparagus, barely cover with water and simmer uncovered 10 minutes or until onion and asparagus are a paste-like consistency. Add milk and stir to form a paste. Stuff and coat the pike with this mixture, sprinkle with salt and pepper and wrap in aluminum foil. Cook over a charcoal fire for 40 minutes, 20 minutes on each side. Open foil at end of cooking and sprinkle with parsley and cheese.
Serves 4.

This is the most beautiful fish I have ever seen. The name in English makes me dream of the harmonies in nature which have taken such a long time to evolve and brings me at last to a sort of total awareness and understanding.

8 fillets of sunfish (2 pounds)   juice of 1/2 lemon
flour   1/2 cup slivered almonds
butter and vegetable oil

Dredge the fillets of sunfish in flour. Brown them in a frying pan in an equal quantity of butter and oil, then let them simmer for 10 to 12 minutes. Lay the fillets on a heated serving dish. Add the lemon juice to the butter and oil mixture and sauté the almonds for a few seconds. Pour this over the sunfish and serve.
Serves 4.

This recipe will please any man, but if it's a day when you feel your man doesn't deserve the extra something, forget the honey.

1 yellow pickerel (2 pounds)
3 tablespoons flour
2 tablespoons brown sugar
butter
cinnamon

cloves
1/2 cup apple juice
1 tablespoon white pasteurized honey
finely grated lemon rind

Wash and dry the pickerel thoroughly and cut it into 4 large pieces. Dredge these in a mixture of the flour and brown sugar. Place them in a well-buttered pan and sprinkle with cinnamon and several cloves. Bake at 350° for 35 minutes. Halfway through the cooking baste the fish with the apple juice sweetened with honey. A touch of grated lemon rind sprinkled over the pickerel will bring out the full flavor.
Serves 4.

Goldeye is found in only a few locations, but is sometimes available at specialty fish markets. If you're lucky enough to catch one, this is a marvelous way of preparing it. If you don't have a goldeye, this is a delicious method of cooking any freshwater fish.

4 goldeye
Court Bouillon (page 10)
4 shallots, finely chopped
2 garlic cloves, crushed
2 tablespoons butter

2 tablespoons vegetable oil
2 celery stalks, well chopped
1 pound fresh tomatoes, peeled and cut
   into eighths

Simmer the fish in Court Bouillon 10 minutes. Meanwhile, fry the shallots and garlic to a golden color in butter and oil. Now add the celery and tomatoes. Cook over medium heat for 15 minutes until the sauce thickens. When the goldeye are cooked to a turn and flaky, remove their bones and place the fish on a serving dish. Complete the sauce by mixing in 1/2 cup of the Court Bouillon. Pour over the fish and serve.
Serves 4 to 6.

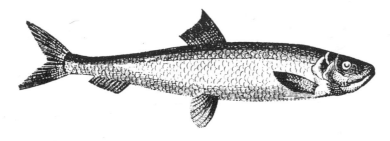

This recipe is a symbol for me of the joy *Grand'mère* always communicated when she cooked. Joy was her testament. (Burbot is a freshwater fish of the cod family.)

3 pounds of burbot	1/4 cup finely chopped freshly boiled
Court Bouillon (page 10)	asparagus
1 cup mayonnaise (page 61)	12 stuffed green olives
1 tablespoon fresh chopped tarragon	1 lemon, sliced

Simmer the burbot in Court Bouillon for a little over an hour and let it cool in the liquid. Meanwhile prepare a homemade mayonnaise to which you add the tarragon and finely chopped asparagus. Serve the burbot decorated with your mayonnaise and surrounded with stuffed olives and lemon slices.
Serves 6.

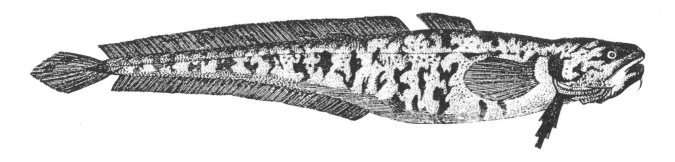

1 ouananiche (3 to 4 pounds) or
   any salmon
6 slices bacon
4 large potatoes, thinly sliced
1 large onion, thinly sliced
parsley
bay leaves

cloves
1/4 pound butter
4 cups milk
paprika
1 large tomato, sliced
1/3 pound mild, white cheddar cheese

Put 2 slices of bacon inside the fish, then place it in a large roasting pan with 2 slices of bacon over it and 2 slices under. Surround the fish with the potato and onion slices. Add the parsley, bay leaves, cloves and the butter in several lumps. Now add the milk, which should almost cover the fish. Sprinkle with paprika and bake in a 350° oven for 1-1/4 to 1-1/2 hours. Fifteen minutes before the dish is cooked, add the sliced tomato and the cheese broken into chunks. Serve and savor.
Serves 4.

The dandelion is the first flower a child gives to its mother, and the mother should always smile and receive it happily. Everyone has dandelions and we should use them instead of treating them as useless weeds.

12 small perch (1/2 pound each)   butter and vegetable oil
1 bunch young dandelion shoots   white wine vinegar
1 garlic clove, finely chopped

Brown the young dandelion shoots in a heavy frying pan in an equal quantity of butter and oil, together with the garlic, and set aside in a warm place. Use the same oil to pan-fry the fish quickly, a few minutes on each side. Add a dash of wine vinegar and serve the perch covered with the dandelions.
Serves 4.

My sister-in-law's name, Marie Mignonne, recurs in my recipes because she has always symbolized happiness to me.

2 pounds perch fillets, 1/2 inch thick   paprika
1/4 pound butter   parsley
3/4 cup fresh cream   lemon slices
4 pieces toast, without crust

Put the perch fillets in an ovenproof dish (do not overlap), dot with lumps of butter and bake them for 10 minutes in a 350° oven. After this first baking, cover the fillets with the cream and return them to the oven for 10 minutes more. Serve on toast, garnished with paprika and fresh parsley and, if you wish, add a few slices of lemon.
Serves 4.

1 muskelunge (5 pounds) or any large
  white fish
6 to 8 thin strips of salt pork
1 green pepper, finely chopped

1 cup finely chopped fresh mushrooms
paprika
fines herbes
grated rind of 1/2 lemon

Wrap the fish with thin strips of salt pork and bake it at 350° for 25 minutes. Remove from oven, turn it over and add the green pepper and mushrooms. Sprinkle over it some paprika, fines herbes and the lemon rind. Return to the 350° oven, bake for another 25 minutes and serve.
Serves 4.

Every winter there is a big festival in the Québec town of Sainte-Anne-de-la-Pérade, when millions of the small fish called tommy-cods are found swimming under the ice. Catching and cooking these fish becomes a 24-hour-a-day carnival that lasts for weeks. This recipe is a popular way of cooking them there, and may also be used for cooking fresh sardines or small perch fillets.

3 pounds tommy-cod, cleaned and washed
2 pounds potatoes
1/2 pound salt pork, cut in cubes
6 medium-size onions, thinly sliced

salt and pepper
butter
paprika

Wash and peel the potatoes and cut them into slices about 1/2 inch thick. Cover the bottom of a large heavy saucepan with the cubes of salt pork. Now add a layer of potatoes, a layer of onion slices and then a layer of fish. Repeat this operation until you have exhausted your supply of fish, potatoes and onions. Season generously with salt and pepper. Cover with big lumps of butter and warm water, and sprinkle with paprika. Simmer over low heat until the potatoes are well done and serve.
Serves 6.

I tried this recipe for the first time with fillets of perch, sunfish and bass after a meagre fishing expedition to the Vaudreuil Canal. The result was a delightful surprise. In these inflationary times this soup will be not only a gourmet's pleasure, but also a necessity for the budget watcher.

4 fillets of perch, sunfish or bass
butter
1 onion, finely chopped
1 tablespoon ketchup
salt and pepper

thyme
parsley
1 potato, cooked and diced
2 tablespoons flour
1/2 cup milk

Brown the fish fillets gently in butter in a heavy frying pan with the onion. Add the ketchup and enough water to cover the fish. Simmer for 15 to 20 minutes, then sprinkle with salt, pepper, thyme and fresh parsley, and add the diced potato. Thicken with the flour mixed with a little water. Add milk and serve.
Serves 4.

Saint Hilaire was a latter-day *coureur-du-bois* (woodsman) who was one of my friends. I used to hunt with him around James Bay and always admired his total communication with the woods and nature.

1 trout (3 pounds
butter
2 garlic cloves, finely chopped
1 small onion, minced
1/2 cup minced chervil

2 tablespoons tomato ketchup
2 tablespoons dehydrated chicken
    concentrate
salt and pepper

Fillet and cut the trout into small pieces. Brown them in butter with the garlic, onion and minced chervil. Cover with 6 to 8 cups of cold water. Add ketchup, chicken concentrate and salt and pepper to taste. Cook at medium heat 12 to 15 minutes and serve. Serves 6.

1 speckled trout (1 pound)	butter
1/8 cup fresh chervil	croûtons
1 tablespoon fines herbes	grated Swiss cheese
2 onions, finely chopped	paprika

Simmer the trout in water to cover for 15 to 20 minutes together with the chervil and fines herbes. Skin and bone the fish, carefully removing all the bones, even the smallest. Reserve the cooking water. Fry the onions gently with a good-sized lump of butter for 15 to 20 minutes or until they are a nice golden brown. Then cover them with the fish cooking water. Now add the pieces of trout. Pour the soup into an ovenproof tureen, cover with croûtons (bread cubes fried in butter) and grated cheese and sprinkle with paprika. Place the dish under the broiler until the cheese is melted and nicely brown, and serve.
Serves 2.

Marie Paule is my mother. I think I started cooking in a reaction against her—like all teenagers—because she was such a bad cook and because—like all teenagers—I wanted to conquer my father.

1 fine speckled trout (2 pounds)	chervil
2 tablespoons olive oil	fines herbes
1 onion, finely chopped	3 tablespoons butter
paprika	2 cups beef consommé

Grease the bottom of an ovenproof dish with olive oil. Lay the trout in it surrounded with the onion. Garnish with paprika, chervil and fines herbes, dot with the butter and bake in a 350° oven for 15 minutes. Add the beef consommé and continue cooking for 15 to 25 minutes more, basting frequently; then serve.
Serves 4.

Personally, I prefer a bed of flowers, but that's when making love is concerned.

1 speckled trout (2 pounds)
butter
1 small onion, finely chopped
3-1/2 cups (1 28-ounce can) baked beans
   with tomatoes

1 tablespoon sugar
salt and pepper
ketchup, to taste

Brown the trout in butter in heavy frying pan together with the onion. Place in an ovenproof dish and add the baked beans, sugar, salt and pepper and ketchup. Bake in a 350° oven for 40 minutes and serve.
Serves 4.

For two happy fishermen (or women). In our world of women's emancipation, I think it is time that women started to experiment and live that ancestral masculine feeling of being two friends alone in the woods just being, without talking.

6 to 8 small brook trout	butter
flour	1/2 cup fresh cream

Dredge the trout lightly with flour. Melt butter in a heavy frying pan over high heat. Brown the trout a few minutes on each side. Just before they have finished cooking, add the cream and let simmer for a few minutes before serving.
Serves 2.

I love marinated fish because it is such a delight to my taste. And it always reminds me as well of my best dinner in a Paris restaurant.

12 small salmon trout (approximately 6 inches)
2 cups dry white wine
1/2 cup cider vinegar
2 large onions, sliced

1 tablespoon salt
6 black peppercorns
4 cloves
2 teaspoons fines herbes or minced chives

Poach the trout in the wine and vinegar with onions, salt, peppercorns, cloves and the herbs or chives, simmering for about 15 minutes. Remove the trout delicately so as not to break them, and place them in a glass or baked-enamel dish. Cover them completely with their cooking stock and let them cool to room temperature. Then cover the dish and put the fish in the refrigerator to marinate for at least 48 hours before serving. Serve as appetizers, 1 per person.

Nativa was my father's mother and her most fantastic success was to be deeply in love with her husband for 40 years. You can use this recipe as a talisman.

4 handsome fillets of shad (about
  2 pounds)
juice of 2 lemons

1/2 pound butter, melted
2 hard-boiled eggs
cayenne pepper

Let the fillets stand in the lemon juice for 25 minutes. Then place them in an ovenproof dish, cover with melted butter and bake them at 350° for 30 minutes. Before serving, decorate the fish with the egg yolks forced through a sieve and the whites sliced into rings. Add a last bright touch with a pinch of cayenne pepper.
Serves 4.

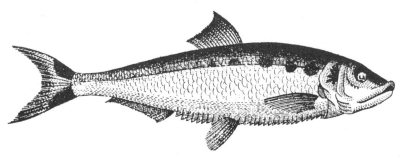

1 large fillet of haddock (about
  2 pounds)
2 large potatoes, peeled and very
  thinly sliced
1/2 pound fresh green beans,
  blanched

2 large onions, very thinly sliced
salt and pepper
butter
paprika
milk

Cut the fillet of haddock into wide strips. Use a glass baking dish or any other large ovenproof pan. Spread a layer of potatoes in the bottom of the dish, season with salt and pepper and add a few small lumps of butter. Then add a layer of beans, a layer of onions and a layer of haddock. Finish off with another layer of potatoes and top with a layer of onions. Season with more salt and pepper, dot with butter, sprinkle with paprika, add enough milk to cover and bake at 350° for 1 hour.
Serves 4.

If you're in love and you're in a hurry (maybe your lover has just come back from the wars) forget the recipe and just buy the best oyster soup you know.

1 fillet of haddock (about 1 pound)	1 potato, peeled, cooked and diced
3 tablespoons butter	1/2 pint oysters
1 small onion, finely chopped	2-1/2 cups milk
fines herbes, minced chives and chervil to taste	3 tablespoons fresh cream

Cut the fillet of haddock into several large pieces and brown in a frying pan with the butter and finely chopped onion. Sprinkle on the herbs and cook for 10 minutes over very low heat. Add the cooked potato, oysters and milk and let simmer a few minutes longer. Finish off by adding cream before serving.
Serves 4.

A psychiatrist friend and I are still looking into what it's all about to be afraid of eels and snakes and other phallic symbols like this—and considering them phallic symbols to begin with is probably oversimplifying matters.

2 pounds eel, cut up or sliced
1 pound fresh tomatoes, peeled
2 large onions, finely chopped
1 green pepper, finely chopped
1 pound fresh mushrooms, sliced
salt and pepper

paprika
fines herbes
butter
1/2 cup white wine, or
   1 cup chicken consommé
grated Parmesan cheese

Cut tomatoes into thick slices. Cover the bottom of an ovenproof dish with half of the tomatoes, onions, pepper and mushrooms. Place the eel over this and sprinkle it with salt, pepper, paprika and fines herbes; then cover it with the rest of the vegetables. Add a few generous tablespoons of butter and the wine or consommé. Bake at 350° for 35 to 40 minutes. Sprinkle with cheese and broil another few minutes before serving.
Serves 4.

I created this recipe just because it was him—just because it was me.

1/2 pound fresh shrimps
1 cup ketchup (preferably homemade)
butter and vegetable oil

1 large garlic clove, crushed
watercress or lettuce

Shell and wash the shrimps; then let them soak for a few minutes in a cup of ketchup. Heat an equal quantity of butter and oil with the garlic in a heavy saucepan over low heat and sauté the shrimp from 5 to 8 minutes. Serve on a bed of watercress or a dainty lettuce leaf. Enjoy well before sleeping.
Serves 2 . . . obviously.

For me shrimps are like human beings—you don't have to know everything about them to love them. This recipe was given to me by *un amant* of Pernod.

Prepare a nicely spiced Court Bouillon (page 10) with thyme, bay leaves and fennel. Simmer the shrimps in this until pink (do not overcook!), shell them and then brown them very lightly in olive oil seasoned with fennel and fresh parsley. Remove the shrimps from the pan and make a sauce by adding to the remaining liquid 1 ounce of Pernod and a little fresh cream. Stir well. Serve the shrimps on steamed rice and pour the sauce over them.

Serves 4 as an appetizer.

I've named this dish and many others "Léopoldine" after myself. Francine is my working name, but Léopoldine is my feminine name. I use it when I cook, paint and make love.

2 large fillets of mackerel (about
   2 pounds)
12 to 16 small fresh shrimps, shelled
1 tomato, finely chopped
1 celery stalk, finely chopped
butter
tarragon, thyme, paprika and
   celery salt

bay leaves
1 small onion, sliced
parsley
1 small piece green pepper, diced
1-1/2 cups beef consommé
grated rind of 1/2 lemon

Line the bottom of an ovenproof dish with the tomato and celery; add a few lumps of butter. Lay the mackerel fillets on this and sprinkle them with tarragon, thyme, paprika and celery salt. Add several bay leaves, the onion slices, a little parsley and the green pepper. Pour on the beef consommé seasoned with the lemon rind. Surround the fish with the shelled shrimps. Finish off with a few dabs of butter. Bake at 350° for 30 minutes.
Serves 4 to 6.

The French word "maquereau" also means a man who takes advantage of women, but this fish isn't likely to take advantage of you.

8 small mackerel   fresh or dried fennel
3 tablespoons olive oil   1 tablespoon Pernod
salt and pepper   1 or 2 lemons, quartered

Pour the oil over the fish, season with salt and pepper and stuff them with fresh fennel or sprinkle with dried fennel. Sprinkle Pernod over them and let them marinate for an hour. Bake at 350° for 30 minutes. Serve with lemon quarters or Pernod Sauce (page 66). Serves 4.

An extraordinary and totally delectable recipe from the chef at Hotel Mont-Albert in the Gaspé.

1 pound cod
1 pound halibut
1 pound sole
1 pound haddock
1 pound salmon
several shrimps and lobster claws,
    unshelled
1-1/2 cups olive oil
2 garlic cloves, crushed
2 cups coarsely chopped celery
2 cups coarsely chopped onions

2 cups coarsely chopped leeks
3-1/2 cups fresh, peeled, cut up
    tomatoes, or
    1 28-ounce can tomatoes
2-1/2 cups (1 20-ounce can) tomato juice
6 cups water
1 bouquet garni (thyme, bay leaves, sage,
    saffron in a cheesecloth bag)
1/2 cup dry white wine
garlic croûtons

In a huge heavy saucepan heat the olive oil and brown in it the garlic, celery, onions and leeks. Then add the tomatoes, tomato juice, water and the bouquet garni. Cut up the cod, halibut, sole, haddock and salmon in pieces (1-1/2 inches wide) and add them to the stock as well as the shrimps and lobster claws. Add the wine. Cook for 25 to 30 minutes, remove bouquet garni, and serve over garlic croûtons (diced French bread fried in garlic butter).
Serves 10 to 12.

2 slices of halibut, 3/4 inch thick   1 small onion, finely chopped
   (2 pounds)   salt and pepper
6 slices of salt pork   1 lemon, sliced
4 tablespoons butter   parsley
2 tablespoons flour

Fry the slices of salt pork in a heavy frying pan. Then add the butter, flour, onion, halibut slices, salt and pepper and a little water. Bake in the oven at 350° for 30 minutes. Before serving decorate with slices of lemon and fresh parsley.
Serves 4.

1 cod (5 to 6 pounds)   Parsley Sauce (page 63)
1 tablespoon salt
1/2 cup vinegar

Place the fish in a large pan with enough water to cover it. Add sufficient salt and vinegar to give the water a good aroma. Simmer gently over low heat until the bone starts to come away when you pull slightly on the tail. Drain and place on a serving dish. Delicious served with Parsley Sauce.
Serves 4 to 6.

3 large fillets of cod (about   4 shallots, finely chopped
  4 pounds)   1-1/2 cups fresh cream
butter   parsley or watercress
1-1/2 cups sliced fresh mushrooms

Fry the cod fillets in butter in a heavy frying pan for a few minutes until they turn a light golden color. Then place them in an ovenproof dish. Add the mushrooms sliced lengthwise and the shallots, dot with more butter and cover with the cream. Bake at 350° for 20 to 25 minutes. Garnish before serving with fresh parsley or watercress. Serves 6.

1 whole cod (1 pound)
Court Bouillon (page 10)
8 medium-size potatoes
1/4 pound butter

1/2 cup hot milk
salt and pepper
chopped parsley

Simmer the whole cod in Court Bouillon about 15 minutes; then remove the bones and skin and mash it. While the cod is cooking, boil and mash the potatoes, adding the butter, milk, salt and pepper and whipping them until they become pure white. Now add the cod to the mashed potatoes and mix well. Put this mixture into an ovenproof dish and bake for 15 to 20 minutes at 350° until a light golden crust forms on top. Just before serving sprinkle with fresh parsley.
Serves 4.

Some people may not like the taste of this combination, but for one who sometimes likes to get away from the gourmet feeling, it's like a nice tomato sandwich before going to bed.

By peeling the potatoes before you bake them, they form a crisp, delicate golden skin. This recipe is equally good with brown bullhead, sunfish, bass or tommy-cod.

1 pound fresh sardines	3 tablespoons tomato paste
4 large potatoes	salt and pepper
1 garlic clove, finely chopped	parsley
3 large celery stalks, finely chopped	oregano
butter and vegetable oil in equal quantities	grated Mozzarella cheese

Peel and wash the potatoes and bake them in a 350° oven for 1 hour. Meanwhile wash the sardines well and remove all the bones. Brown the garlic and celery in the butter and oil in a heavy frying pan over medium heat. Add the sardines and fry them briefly on both sides, then lower the heat and add the tomato paste. Stir well until the mixture has the consistency of thin mashed potatoes and simmer 15 to 20 minutes. Season with salt, pepper, parsley and oregano. When the potatoes are done remove from the oven, cut them in half and gently scoop out the insides. Mash and mix insides with the sardine sauce. Stuff the potato cases with this mixture and top with the cheese, to taste. Put under broiler for 3 minutes and serve.

Serves 4.

2 fillets of sole (1/2 pound each)   Tomato Sauce (page 68)
1 lemon, quartered
6 bay leaves

Simmer the fillets for 10 minutes in enough water to cover, together with the quartered lemon and bay leaves. Serve with Tomato Sauce.
Serves 4.

2 pounds sole fillets
4 finely chopped shallots
butter
1 cup water

2 cups milk
4 tablespoons chervil
salt and pepper

Cut the fillets in small pieces and brown them with the shallots in a heavy frying pan in a generous amount of butter. Add the water, milk, chervil and simmer at medium heat for 10 to 12 minutes. Season with salt and pepper and serve hot.
Serves 4.

When you have read the books of Roderick Haig-Brown on the subject of salmon, you'll know that the name "interlake" is not a biologist's statement but a poetic name.

1 salmon (3 pounds)   juice of 1/2 lemon
1 small onion, finely chopped   paprika
1 7-ounce can shrimps (drain and   butter
   reserve juice)   Martha Sauce (page 64)
2 to 3 tablespoons seafood cocktail
   sauce

Combine the onion, shrimps and seafood sauce and stuff the salmon with the mixture. Sprinkle salmon with lemon juice and paprika and add several lumps of butter. Wrap in greased aluminium foil and cook over a charcoal fire for 1-1/2 hours turning it every 20 minutes. (If using an oven, bake at 350° for 50 minutes.) Serve with rice and Martha Sauce.
Serves 6.

My father gave me this recipe when I published my first book, but it's as if it came from my son because I am the one who taught my father to cook.

The tail is the firmest part of the salmon, therefore the best. It needs no elaborate preparation for it is delicious by itself. But be careful not to confuse this part of the salmon's anatomy with the inedible tail fin. The tail of the salmon is the cone-shaped end of its body.

1 piece of salmon tail (1-1/2 pounds)
1 lemon, quartered
8 bay leaves

Plunge the salmon tail into a saucepan of boiling water in which you have put the lemon quarters and the bay leaves, and simmer for 20 to 30 minutes. Drain and serve.
Serves 2.

1 small whole salmon (2 pounds)
1 small onion, cut up
Léopoldine Sauce (page 69)

Simmer the salmon with the onion in water for 30 minutes. Serve with Léopoldine Sauce.
Serves 4.

This is a simple, but delectable way of using leftover salmon and Martha Sauce (page 64). If you're feeling very lazy or mad at your husband, you can substitute the packaged macaroni-and-cheese mix you keep hidden in the back of your kitchen cabinet! It will still be quite good.

Cook some macaroni (about a cup per person) and combine it with pieces of the leftover salmon, remains of the Martha Sauce, butter and cheese. Garnish with parsley and some little croûtons fried with garlic. Then heat for a few minutes in a 350° oven before serving.

Serves 3 to 4.

FISH SAUCES

You may never have thought of making mayonnaise or you may never have tried because you've been told it's impossible to succeed. But take courage and go ahead because I believe that what makes you fail at a task is believing that you will fail.

2 egg yolks
olive oil (1/2 to 1 cup)

1 garlic clove, crushed (optional)
1 teaspoon Court Bouillon (optional)

Place the egg yolks in a small bowl and leave at room temperature for 2 hours. (Never believe you will make a good mayonnaise with cold eggs.) Add olive oil, drop by drop, very slowly, beating constantly with a whisk until the desired consistency is reached. Then add crushed garlic if you wish. When serving this mayonnaise with poached fish, you may add some of the Court Bouillon in which the fish was poached.

This is one of the basic fish sauces, but I consider it a relative of fish and chips or coleslaw and it doesn't talk to my feelings.

1/2 cup watercress
2 small sweet pickled cucumbers,
   finely chopped
3 large stuffed olives, finely chopped

10 capers
onion salt
1 cup mayonnaise (page 61)

With a pair of scissors, cut up the leaves and stems of the watercress until very fine. Add the remaining ingredients and mix well with the mayonnaise. Serve cold.
Makes 1-1/4 cups.

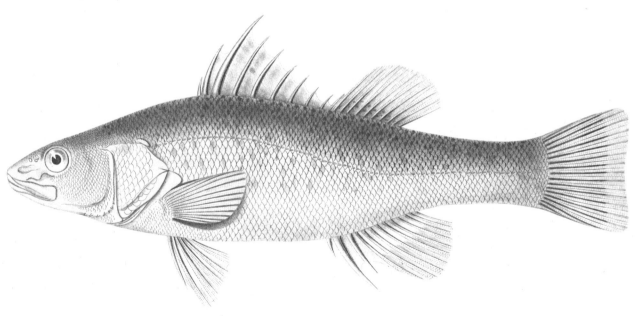

I have always been in love with parsley because I have always been in love with green plants and flowers. For me a kitchen that doesn't have a fresh bunch of parsley in a glass of water is not really a kitchen.

1/2 cup fresh parsley sprigs
1 pound butter

Wash the parsley and boil it in salted water for 5 to 6 minutes. Drain and chop fine. Melt butter until it is very hot and a golden color. Add parsley and serve. Pepper fanciers may add a few pinches of freshly ground pepper.
Makes 2 cups.

This sauce, which is particularly easy to make, has a lovely velvety quality. Martha is the name of a friend of mine and I give this sauce her name because of her velvety qualities and because I admire her ability to sail, which is the art of the contrary.

1/2 pound fresh mushrooms, sliced
1 small onion, chopped
1 large lump of butter
juice from 1 7-ounce can of shrimps
1 cup chicken stock

1 tablespoon flour
1 can rolled anchovies
finely chopped fresh parsley
1/2 cup fresh light cream

Fry the mushrooms and onion in a generous amount of butter. (Be careful to keep the heat low!) Add the juice from the shrimps and the chicken stock. Bring to a boil, reduce heat and simmer 5 minutes. Make a paste of the flour and a little hot mixture and add slowly to simmering mixture, stirring constantly. Drain the anchovies and add them to the sauce along with the parsley. Then 5 to 10 minutes before serving, stir in the cream. (Do *not* boil.)

Personally, eggs make me sick, but I have at home a beautiful turquoise onyx egg which has helped me through a lot of anxiety and depression just by the feel of it when I touch it, so choose carefully the type of egg you want and why. You can add a can of rolled anchovies and some capers to this recipe and come up with a sauce for an elegant dinner.

1 tablespoon butter
1 tablespoon flour
1 cup Court Bouillon (page 10)

salt and pepper
3 hard-boiled eggs, sliced
parsley

In a heavy saucepan, melt butter over medium heat and stir in the flour until the mixture reaches a smooth consistency. Add the Court Bouillon, stirring constantly and simmer for 5 to 8 minutes. Season, using the salt generously and the pepper gently. Just before serving add the hard-boiled egg slices, and garnish with parsley.

2 egg yolks   1/4 cup olive oil
2 teaspoons dry mustard   1-1/2 tablespoons Pernod
salt and pepper

Put the egg yolks in a bowl, add the mustard, salt and pepper and mix well. Set the bowl in a saucepan of boiling water over low heat. Stir rapidly with a little whisk while pouring in the oil in a slow steady stream. The sauce thickens very quickly. When it is smooth and velvety, remove the bowl from the saucepan, add the Pernod, beat the sauce thoroughly and serve with the fish.

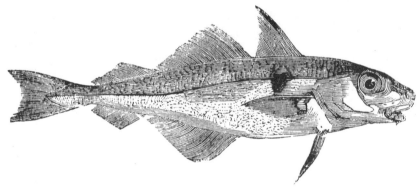

A zest of tenderness, many pinches of friendship—these are things which make life piquant.

2 tablespoons butter
2 tablespoons flour
1-1/2 cups Court Bouillon (page 10)
salt and pepper

1 egg yolk, well beaten
2 tablespoons lemon juice
2 tablespoons finely chopped pickled
  gherkins

Over medium heat, melt the butter and stir in the flour. Then gradually add the Court Bouillon while stirring constantly. Let this cook over a very low heat for 8 to 10 minutes, while continuing to stir, until sauce has thickened. Add salt and pepper to taste. Before serving pour the hot sauce over the beaten egg yolk and mix thoroughly. Then mix in the lemon juice and the finely chopped gherkins.
Makes approximately 2 cups.

1 5-ounce can tomato paste
2 garlic cloves, crushed
grated rind of 1 lemon

1 teaspoon Tabasco sauce
minced parsley

Dilute the tomato paste with a little water and add the garlic, lemon rind, Tabasco sauce and fresh parsley. Serve cold or heat and serve hot, according to your own taste.

I've told you before that one of my names is Léopoldine. It is also my Grandmother's name, and I use it in her honor to name some of the special treasures in my recipe collection.

2 egg yolks
olive oil (1/2 to 1 cup)
1 garlic clove, crushed

parsley
oregano
2 tablespoons tomato paste

Let the egg yolks come to room temperature and, stirring in the olive oil drop by drop, whip them up into a mayonnaise. Add the garlic, parsley, oregano and tomato paste and mix well. Refrigerate for 20 to 30 minutes before using.

WILDFOWL

La Sauvagine is the pretty word we use in Québec to designate all wildfowl.

From the rash and arrogant white geese that stretch out in long lines above Cap Tourmente in October like ribbons of a bridal veil . . .

To the foolhardy teal of the Lac des Deux Montagnes or Lac Saint-Pierre, which every year at the opening of the hunting season demonstrate their prodigious naiveté by landing in the midst of a flock of wooden companions . . .

To the maddening and drunken partridge that flies up in your face and freezes the blood of even the hardiest nimrod with fright and surprise . . .

To the cruel and proud pheasant so ferocious that when he is raised in captivity his beak has to be cut so he will not destroy his fellow males . . .

To the subtle and marvelously clever black duck that knows better than the most experienced hunter the exact range of a shotgun shell.

Unfortunately, if the word wildfowl evokes memories of unforgettable sunrises, of bringing down two birds with one shot, of long motionless hours spent in a blind, it also means for many hunters' wives a recurring source of trouble.

I say "unfortunately" because there is nothing easier or more agreeable than to treat your dinner guests to a green-winged teal, a duck cooked with autumn peaches or a *Pigeon Saint-Hubert.*

The recipes I present here have been chosen for their simplicity as well as for easy preparation. If you know how to boil an egg you can make a success of the most elegant of the game recipes that follow. The basic principles are extremely simple.

It is not necessary to hang wildfowl for days and weeks. Most cookbooks recommend this because the majority of our recipes for game come from France or were written at a time when the first settlers could shoot ducks or partridge practically from their doorstep or in the barnyard and the birds were so fresh as to require aging. But your bird will usually be sufficiently hung and ready for cooking 12 to 24 hours after it has been shot. If I insist on this point it is because I have seen far too many people literally throwing away game. Of course it is alright to hang a bird from 20 to 40 hours, but one must always count the time of hanging as beginning precisely at the time the bird was shot.

It may be a matter of taste how long a bird should be hung, but of one thing I am certain—game birds are always best when cooked in the oven and left uncovered.

To prevent drying out, fowl should not be plucked and drawn until just before you plan to cook them (instructions for cleaning are given on page 139).

Never try to adapt a recipe which is meant for domestic fowl, for example a Brome Lake or Long Island duck, to cooking a wild bird.

All game birds are delicious when cooked with fruit—pineapple, cherries, oranges, tangerines, grapes or plums.

If you are improvising when cooking fowl, it's always good to add something sweet like apple juice, honey, cinnamon or maple syrup. Juniper berries are also delicious with all fowl.

Contrary to certain culinary opinions, I prefer not to wrap the bird with strips of fat even if its flesh is very dry. Butter gives a better result than salt pork when it comes to browning the bird, and fruit juice gives a delicious flavor, if it is used to baste a bird in the oven.

When roasting fowl, always add a carrot to absorb the grease in the roasting pan.

Two separate cookings enhance the taste of all wildfowl. This helps to relax the muscles developed during their active life. For example, if you are having a party on Saturday, do the first cooking on Friday. Let the fowl "relax" at room temperature; then put it in the refrigerator and finish the cooking the next day.

Slow cooking is the criterion for success. The slower the bird cooks, the better it will taste.

When a bird is well cooked, its flesh will come away easily from the bones.

This recipe provides you with the main course for what could be one of the most elegant dinners you have ever served.

8 Virginia bobwhite or quail
4 tablespoons butter
2 cups beef stock, or
    1 10-ounce can beef consommé,
    diluted
1 cup apple juice or cider

fines herbes
pepper
cinnamon
2 to 3 tablespoons flour
1 pound fresh mushrooms, finely
    chopped

Fry the quails to a golden brown in the butter, using a baked enamel or cast-iron pan. Add the beef stock or consommé and the apple juice or cider. Season moderately, cover and cook over a low heat for 1-1/2 hours.

Halfway through the cooking, stir in 2 to 3 tablespoons of flour which has first been mixed with a little of the cooking liquid. If the sauce is too thick, thin it by adding a little more consommé, apple juice or cider. Fifteen minutes before the end of the cooking time, brown the mushrooms in a little more butter and add them to the dish. Serves 4.

I've never understood the terrible prejudice against the pigeon because eating it is really a delightful, gastronomic experience. People say that city pigeons are dirty birds. Do we say that people who live in the city are dirty people? To honor the pigeon, therefore, I've given this recipe the name of the patron saint of hunters.

9 pigeons
pinch each tarragon, chives, parsley and
   rosemary
4 tablespoons butter
4 shallots, minced

1-1/2 cups beef consommé
1 cup apple juice
1/4 cup dry white wine
1/2 pound fresh mushrooms
2 teaspoons flour

Rub the pigeons with the herbs, then sauté them in butter in a heavy saucepan with the shallots until they are a nice golden color. Pour over them the consommé and let simmer over low heat for 1 hour. Add the apple juice and the white wine, and continue cooking for 1 more hour. Meanwhile cook the mushrooms in more butter and add them to the dish at the very last minute. If necessary, thicken the sauce slightly with 2 teaspoons of flour before serving.
Serves 6 (1-1/2 birds per person).

This dish can be used as a first course, as a main course if you double the quantity, or as a stuffing for wild goose. Garnish with fresh parsley or watercress.

2 pigeon breasts, cooked, boned and diced
1/2 cup wild rice
pinch each tarragon, rosemary and
   dried mint
2 cups warm water
1/2 cup white rice

1 tablespoon crushed juniper berries
   (optional)
2 large, juicy apples, peeled and cut into
   small pieces
butter
pinch cinnamon
4 shallots, finely chopped

Soak the wild rice and herbs in warm water for 3 hours. Then cook in same water for 45 minutes. Mix in the raw white rice 10 to 12 minutes before the end of the cooking period. Rinse cooked rice under cold water and drain. Put the cooked rice into a large bowl and mix in the diced pigeon breasts and the juniper berries. Sauté the cut-up apples in a large frying pan with butter, cinnamon and shallots. Lower heat and continue cooking for 5 to 7 minutes. Add the rice and pigeon mixture and mix in. Heat thoroughly.
Serves 6.

This dish is meant, of course, to be prepared outdoors. Draw the partridge without plucking it. Take a clod of earth and moisten it with spirits. Knead the earth like a pie dough and wrap the bird in it. Dig a hole in the ground and build a good fire in it. When you have red coals, bury the partridge in them and cover it with some dry branches and a little more earth. Half an hour later take it out. You will find that it is cooked to a turn and perfectly plucked.

PARTRIDGE WITH RICE

4 partridge
4 strips of pork fat
2 cups beef or chicken stock
1 cup dry white wine
6 juniper berries
thyme

bay leaves
rosemary
salt and pepper
1/2 pound rice (1 heaping cup)
1/4 pound butter
1 tablespoon flour

Wrap the partridge with thin strips of pork fat. Roast them in a 350° oven for 45 minutes, then cut them into pieces. Put to one side in a warm place the legs, wings and breasts. Now cook the carcasses and necks in the stock together with the white wine, juniper berries, thyme, bay leaves and rosemary. Simmer for 45 minutes. Taste before adding salt and pepper. Strain the stock, bring it back to a boil, add the rice, cover, reduce heat to low and steam for about 20 minutes. Strain off stock and reserve. Add half the butter to the rice. Grease a baking dish, line the bottom with half of the rice, then place on it the pieces of partridge that were put aside. Cover them with the rest of the rice and bake for 15 minutes in a very hot oven. Meantime, heat up the stock in which you have cooked the rice. Thicken it by adding one tablespoon of flour which you have worked into the rest of the butter. Pour this sauce over the rice before serving. Serves 4.

I don't know why, but on this continent the only people who really know about mushrooms seem to be immigrants. If you're lucky enough to have a Ukrainian, Russian or Polish friend who knows about mushrooms, forget the partridge and discover the fantastic world of mushrooms—and don't forget that since the beginning of time mushrooms have been known to be mind expanders.

2 partridge
freshly ground pepper
chopped parsley
curry powder
3 tablespoons butter

1 cup hard apple cider (3 percent alcohol)
1 pound fresh mushrooms, finely chopped
2 to 3 tablespoons flour
1 cup fresh cream
croûtons (fried bread cubes)

Sprinkle the partridge generously with pepper, parsley and curry powder, to taste. Brown them in the butter in an ovenproof skillet; then add the cider. Cover and bake for 1-1/2 to 2 hours at 325°. Remove partridge from the pan and sauté the mushrooms in the pan juices. Sprinkle in the flour to make a paste and slowly add the cream, stirring until thickened. Serve the partridge with the mushroom sauce and golden brown croûtons.
Serves 2.

From a hunting point of view, I hate partridge for a very simple reason. When you hunt moose you meet a lot of partridge, but when you hunt partridge you don't meet either partridge or moose.

6 partridge   4 tablespoons butter
grape leaves   1/2 cup Cognac
6 small strips of pork fat   1 pound green grapes, peeled and seeded

Wash and wipe grape leaves and wrap the partridge in them; then wrap with a strip of pork fat. Secure each bird with a string or coarse thread. Sauté them in hot butter in a Dutch oven or a cast-iron pot for about 10 minutes. When they have reached a nice golden color, flambé them with Cognac, then let them cook slowly for 50 minutes. Take the partridge out of the pot and keep warm. Peel and seed the grapes and sauté them in the same pot for 10 minutes. Remove the wrapping from the partridge, cut them in two and serve them surrounded with the grapes.
Serves 6.

It's your wedding anniversary? Your husband is a hunter? You're a working "slave-liberated" woman? It's Monday and you have to wash the clothes? Well here's the recipe you need.

2 partridge
fines herbes and dried chives
butter

1 package dehydrated onion soup
1/4 head of cabbage, coarsely chopped

Sprinkle the partridge with herbs and chives, then sauté them in butter until the skin turns crisp and golden. Cover them with the onion soup and cabbage. Bake in a 325° oven uncovered for 1-1/2 to 2 hours, then serve.
Serves 2.

When I want to honor the wine gods I know that I have to offer them, on the altar of my pleasure, my best wine and my last partridge.

3 partridge	4 bay leaves
flour	2 tablespoons chopped parsley
2 tablespoons butter	1 cup bouillon
12 small onions	1/2 cup dry white wine
pinch thyme	salt
2 tablespoons chopped celery leaves	

Skin the partridge, then dredge them with flour and brown them in the butter. Place them so as to make a triangle in a baked-enamel pan with the onions and herbs in the center. Add the bouillon and the wine. Season with salt, cover the pan and cook over a low heat for 2 hours. If you choose to omit the wine and replace it with more bouillon and the juice of 1 lemon this will give you braised partridge, but you will not have paid homage to those wine gods.
Serves 3.

If you are a traditionalist this recipe goes with your approach to life. If you're not sure what you are, read through the other partridge recipes before you try this one.

1 partridge
1 small veal knuckle
1 onion, cut up
1 bouquet garni (thyme, parsley, bay
   leaves in a cheesecloth bag)
4 large carrots, finely chopped

2 celery stalks, finely chopped
1/4 head of cabbage, finely chopped
salt and pepper
pinch each parsley, chervil and
   fines herbes

Gently boil the partridge together with the veal knuckle, the onion and the bouquet garni in enough water to cover for approximately 45 minutes. Pour off the broth into another pot, then carve the partridge into small pieces, removing all the bones. Put the meat back into the broth. Add the carrots, celery and cabbage and cook slowly for 15 to 20 minutes or until the vegetables are done. Sprinkle with salt, pepper, parsley, chervil and herbs. Let stand 5 minutes before serving.
Serves 4.

I prefer partridge in nature when it's their own "hunting season" and the call of the courting male booms through the brush making your heart beat so fast that you think you will have a heart attack. It is only after that experience that they can be appreciated in cream.

2 partridge   2 tablespoons lemon juice
2 small strips of pork fat   2 pieces toast
grape leaves   watercress or parsley
4 tablespoons butter   paprika
2 cups fresh cream, warmed

Wrap the partridge in thin strips of pork fat, then in grape leaves and tie them up with string. In a skillet cook them slowly in butter for about 1 hour. Halfway through the cooking start adding, a little at a time, the cream and at the very end add the lemon juice. Place the partridge on slices of crisp toast and pour the sauce over them. Garnish with watercress or parsley and brighten up the dish with a pinch of paprika.
Serves 2.

This recipe is a very conventional way of approaching partridge cooking, but like the conventional approach to making love it's such a nice thing, too.

4 partridge
1/4 pound butter
2 thin slices fresh pork
8 small pork sausages
3 or 4 tablespoons flour
1-1/4 cups beef or chicken stock

4 carrots, sliced
1 small cabbage, cut into chunks
salt and pepper
fines herbes
chives

In a saucepan sauté the partridge in butter together with the slices of fresh pork. Add the sausages and sauté them very lightly. Remove the meat and sprinkle the bottom of your saucepan with a little flour. Stir in the stock and then add the remaining ingredients. Simmer for 20 minutes. Put the partridge, pork and sausages back into the saucepan and let this simmer very gently over low heat for 1-1/2 to 2 hours. Serve with mashed potatoes.
Serves 4 hungry gourmets.

At one time I didn't like pheasant, but I tried to find a way to like that meat. One day I was cooking some and accidentally dropped half a bottle of cinnamon in the sauce. After that I liked pheasant, so I always cook mine now with cinnamon.

1 pheasant
cinnamon
minced chives
pepper
fines herbes
butter

12 juniper berries (optional)
4 shallots, finely chopped
1 to 2 cups onion soup
1 cup dry white wine
Scotch whisky

Rub the bird inside and out with a generous amount of powdered cinnamon. Sprinkle with chives, pepper and fines herbes and brown the pheasant in a heavy ovenproof saucepan on all sides in a good-sized lump of butter. Add the juniper berries, shallots and onion soup, then roast in a 325° oven for 1-1/2 hours. Watch the cooking carefully and baste as needed with dry white wine. If there is too little sauce, add another cup of onion soup.

Remove bird from pan, cut into 4 pieces and return to pan so that the meat soaks in the sauce while you continue roasting it another 30 minutes. Serve on a bed of fluffy white rice or on wild rice (which is even better), and flambé with Scotch whisky.
Serves 2.

1 pheasant
1/4 pound smoked pork, cut into cubes
1 small onion, chopped
1 garlic clove, crushed
2 tablespoons olive oil

2 tablespoons butter
5 green apples, peeled, cored and cut up
2 or 3 ounces Cointreau
1 cup fresh table cream
salt and pepper

Sauté the smoked pork, onion and garlic in a heavy frying pan in the butter and oil. When they are well done remove them and put them to one side. In the same pan brown the pheasant. Then remove it and keep it warm. Sprinkle the apples with Cointreau and brown them, in the same way; remove the apples from the pan. Spoon off the excess fat from the sauce remaining in the pan. Place the pheasant back in the pan surrounded with the diced pork, apples, garlic and onion. Cook over a very low heat for a few minutes, then add the cream and season with salt and pepper. Bake in a 325° oven for 2 hours or until the meat is tender. Strain the sauce which will be quite thick now, and pour it over the pheasant before serving.
Serves 2 to 3.

Why a cock pheasant? Because I prefer males.

1 large cock pheasant	1/2 head of cabbage, cut up
butter	2 cups croûtons (fried bread cubes)
4 pork sausages	fines herbes
1/2 cup diced salt pork	chives, finely chopped

Simmer the pheasant uncovered for 3 hours in water to which you have added a generous lump of butter, the sausages, diced salt pork and cabbage. Take out the bird, remove the meat from the bones, cut it into small pieces and return it to the pot. Cook for another 15 minutes with the croûtons. Serve hot sprinkled with herbs and chives. Serves 6.

This recipe was given to me by my friend Dr. Gerald Blackburn, an avid gourmet and hunter. Instead of the duck, any game bird can be used. Pheasant, wild goose or partridge gives magnificent results.

2 pounds wild duck meat, including the
   giblets
1/2 pound veal
1/2 pound pork liver
1/2 pound pork
2 onions, cut up
1/2 pound fresh mushrooms
2 slices bread, soaked in milk
1 cup dry white wine

2 eggs
1 cup fresh cream
1 cup beef consommé
dash thyme
4 garlic cloves, crushed
salt and pepper
1/2 pound bacon
powdered bay leaves

Pass the duck meat, giblets, veal, pork liver, pork, onions and mushrooms through a meat grinder. Put the bread through the grinder (which helps clean it) and combine with the ground meat. Add half the wine and the remaining ingredients except the bacon and bay leaves. Put this mixture again through the grinder. Line the bottom of several molds (4 to 8 inches wide) with strips of bacon and sprinkle with powdered bay leaves. Fill the molds with the meat mixture and pour the remaining wine over each one. Cover with aluminum foil and bake at 350° for 1 hour for the small pâtés and 1-1/2 hours for the larger ones. Remove the foil a few minutes before the end of the baking time to let a nice brown crust form on top. These gourmet treats can be frozen for as long as 6 months and still keep all their freshness.

Mother Fleury is a nickname for a man with whom I made a film about hunting on James Bay. The name comes from his easy-going and uncomplicated attitude to life (and cooking)—you put everything in the same pan and you wait.

4 black ducks, cleaned
rosemary and tarragon
1/4 pound butter
3 shallots, chopped
1 leek, coarsely chopped
2 celery stalks, coarsely chopped

3 apples, cored and coarsely chopped
1 tablespoon chopped parsley
1 package dehydrated onion soup
1 20-ounce can peaches
4 bay leaves
12 juniper berries (optional)

Use a deep ovenproof pan, like a Dutch oven, preferably one with a lid. First rub the ducks well with rosemary and tarragon. Then brown them in butter with the shallots. Remove ducks from the pan and sauté the leek, celery, apples and parsley in the butter. Leave half of these vegetables in the pan and place the ducks on top. Cover them completely with the other half of the vegetables, then add the onion soup, peaches with their juice, bay leaves and juniper berries. Cover and bake in a 350° oven for 3 hours. If the recipe is done successfully, the meat should come away from the bones easily.
Serves 6 to 8.

A duck hunter who has never in his life seen thousands of ducks in flight at Cap Tourmente near Montmagny on the north shore of the St. Lawrence River . . . well, he just can't say he is a hunter yet.

4 handsome black ducks	2 small onions, cut up
1/4 pound butter	1 large carrot, cut up
6 shallots, chopped	few juniper berries (optional)
2 tablespoons olive oil	4 large oranges
4 bay leaves	cinnamon, rosemary and tarragon

Brown the ducks in a large frying pan with butter and shallots until all the blood is cooked. Meanwhile, pour the olive oil into a roasting pan, then put in the bay leaves, onions, carrot, juniper berries and 1 of the oranges, unpeeled and cut into fine slices. Sprinkle the ducks with cinnamon, rosemary and tarragon; place the birds in the pan with the vegetables. Roast in the oven at 350° for 3 hours, basting frequently with the juice of the 3 remaining oranges. Strain the sauce. Serve with garden peas and whipped potatoes.
Serves 4.

Black ducks . . . ten years of beautiful scenarios, ten years of fantastic hunting seasons, ten years of feeling what Hemingway was feeling when he was hunting in the lagoons of the Tagliamento near Venice.

6 ducks	4 bay leaves
2 small onions, cut up	celery leaves
1 large carrot, cut up	1 14-ounce can peaches
2 tablespoons olive oil	cinnamon and rosemary
1/4 pound butter	gin, Cognac or Grand Marnier

Into a large roasting pan put the onions, carrot, olive oil, butter, bay leaves, celery leaves and drained peaches (keeping the juice for basting); then put in the ducks, well-sprinkled with cinnamon and rosemary. Bake uncovered in a 350° oven for 2-1/2 to 3 hours. Four to 6 times during the cooking, baste with the juice of the canned peaches. Strain the sauce before serving. Flambé with gin, Cognac or Grand Marnier, and pour sauce over ducks. Serve with browned potatoes.
Serves 6 to 8.

2 large black ducks
celery salt
paprika
pepper
fennel
12 juniper berries (optional)
2 tablespoons olive oil
2 small onions, cut up

4 bay leaves
thyme
tarragon
1 14-ounce can sliced pineapple
3 celery stalks, coarsely chopped
1/2 cup dry white wine
rum (optional)

Rub the duck with celery salt, paprika and black pepper. In a large roasting pan put the fennel, juniper berries, olive oil, onions, bay leaves, thyme, tarragon and half the slices of pineapple, and place the ducks on top of these ingredients. Roast the ducks at 350° for 3 hours. Check the cooking frequently and gradually add the rest of the pineapple slices, their juice and the celery. Strain the sauce and stir in the wine. Carve the ducks and place the pieces over the slices of pineapple. If you feel so inspired, flambé with a little rum.
Serves 4 famished people.

Whatever you know or say about mallard you must admit that he is the most beautiful of ducks, and because he's the most beautiful he deserves the delicacy of black cherries.

2 large mallard ducks

2 tablespoons olive oil

2 small onions, cut up

4 bay leaves

12 juniper berries (optional)

1 14-ounce can sweetened black cherries

4 teaspoons fines herbes

In a roasting pan place the olive oil, onions, bay leaves, juniper berries and half of the cherries and half their juice. Sprinkle the ducks generously with the herbs and add them to the pan.

Roast in the oven at 350° for 3 hours, basting frequently with the rest of the cherry juice. Strain the sauce and add the remaining cherries just before serving.

Serves 4 healthy appetites.

I don't like the English expression "leftover." Why shouldn't we say "rightover," because it's such a nice thing to have a remembrance of yesterday's delight.

2 cups cooked duck meat, chopped (If
  you're in the mood, shred the meat
  instead of chopping it.)
3 tablespoons olive oil
1 tablespoon vinegar
pinch each salt, pepper, rosemary and
  sugar

2 celery stalks, diced
4 shallots, finely chopped
1/2 head of lettuce, shredded
4 tangerines, peeled and divided into
  segments
20 small stuffed olives
parsley

Combine olive oil, vinegar, salt, pepper, rosemary and sugar. Add the celery, shallots and duck meat and let stand. Just before serving add the lettuce and the tangerines. Garnish with stuffed olives and a little fresh parsley.
Serves 4.

To make this even fancier add one chopped apple and a pinch of cinnamon just before serving.

3 cups cooked white rice
1 celery stalk, finely chopped
2 duck breasts, cooked, boned and diced
1 tablespoon fines herbes

1 teaspoon curry powder
2 tablespoons butter
1/2 cup green grapes, halved and seeded

In a bowl, mix together the cooked rice, celery, duck meat, herbs, curry powder and any leftover sauce from the duck. Let stand for 2 hours. Then sauté this mixture in a heavy frying pan in the butter over very low heat, adding the green grapes at the very end. Serve with the vegetable of your choice or, in smaller quantity, as an accompaniment to wildfowl.

Serves 4 to 6.

I just love teal and to explain that love would be as difficult as to explain a love affair.

4 teal
fines herbes
savory
chervil
minced chives
butter
16 small damson plums, stoned

2 tablespoons juniper berries (optional)
1 cup prune juice
2 cups water
pepper
watercress
2 ounces gin

Sprinkle the birds with the herbs and spices and brown them well in butter for 8 to 10 minutes; then remove them from the pan. In the same butter put half the plums, then the birds, then the other half of the plums on top with the juniper berries. Pour over them the prune juice and 1 cup of the water. Keep on basting frequently during the whole cooking time with the remaining cup of water. Season with the pepper. Simmer gently for 2 hours, uncovered, so that the strong flavor of the prune juice will evaporate slowly. Remove from heat, cut the birds in half and place them on a platter on a bed of watercress. Pour a little of the sauce over the meat, then flambé with the gin.

Serves 8 as a first course. For a full-course meal allow a minimum of 1-1/2 teal per person; that is, 9 birds for 6 guests, and serve with Rice Bonne Femme (page 107).

I think life could be termed a success if it started with ambition and ended with the pleasure of watching the return of the blue-winged teal in spring.

6 teal
butter
2 shallots, finely chopped
1 tablespoon olive oil
1 orange, peeled and sliced, and the
   orange peel
pepper

minced chives
fines herbes
1 small onion, cut up
1 large carrot, cut up
4 bay leaves
1 8-ounce can mandarin oranges
white wine or cider

Nicely brown the birds in butter together with the shallots. Cover the bottom of a roasting pan with olive oil, then spread out the orange slices on the bottom of the pan. Place the birds on the orange slices and surround them with the orange peel. Sprinkle with pepper, chives and fines herbes. Add the onion, carrot, bay leaves and half the mandarin oranges with their juice. Roast in a 350° oven for a minimum of 2 hours. Halfway through the cooking add the rest of the mandarin oranges and the wine or cider. Strain the sauce before serving.
Serves 4.

1 goose carcass (6- to 7-pound bird)
2 or 3 tablespoons powdered chicken
   concentrate
1 cup beef consommé

pinch each salt, pepper, parsley, chives,
   chervil and fines herbes
1 cup sherry (optional)

Cover the carcass of the goose almost completely with cold water, preferably using the pan in which the goose was cooked, and boil it at a very high heat from 15 to 20 minutes. Strain the broth, add the chicken concentrate and beef consommé and season it with your choice of the herbs listed. To enrich the flavor you may add the sherry. Serves 8.

1 large Canada goose (6 to 7 pounds)
6 medium-size unpeeled apples, coarsely
  cut
16 juniper berries (optional)
salt and pepper, to taste

1/4 cup Cognac
1/4 pound butter
2 tablespoons dry mustard
dash thyme
bay leaves

In a large bowl, mix by hand the apples, juniper berries, salt and pepper and half the Cognac. Then stuff the bird with half of this mixture. Put the bird in a roasting pan and surround it with the other half of the apple mixture.

Make a paste with butter and mustard and coat the goose generously with the mixture. Add bay leaves, salt, pepper and thyme. Roast in a 350° oven for 3-1/2 hours. Check the cooking frequently. If the bird becomes too dry, turn it over or cover the pan with a lid. Baste regularly with remaining Cognac mixed with an equal quantity of water. Add water or fruit juice of any type if more liquid is needed.

Serves 4.

SAUTÉED APPLES TO ACCOMPANY A ROAST GOOSE

4 large apples
1/2 pound butter

3/4 cup sugar
1 teaspoon cinnamon

Peel and core the apples, then cut them into 1/2-inch slices. Sauté them in melted butter with sugar and cinnamon over low heat for 10 to 12 minutes and serve.

Serves 4 to 6.

1 snow goose (5 pounds)
2 cups olive oil
1 cup red wine
1 onion, cut up
1 carrot, cut up
1/4 cup chopped chives
pinch fines herbes

dash thyme
4 bay leaves
flour
butter
4 cups beef stock
Cognac

Cut the goose into quarters. Place goose in a large baked-enamel pan with the olive oil, wine, onion, carrot and herbs. Put the dish in the refrigerator and let the goose marinate for 8 hours. Remove the meat from the marinade, wipe it dry and dredge it lightly with flour. Then sauté it in butter in a large frying pan over a high heat for 5 to 8 minutes. Now, reserving the marinade, place the 4 pieces of meat back into your baked-enamel pan. Add the butter from the frying pan and the beef stock. Cover and cook over low heat. Halfway through the cooking add 2 or 3 tablespoons of the marinade. Count at least 2-1/2 hours cooking time, possibly longer—the goose is cooked when the meat comes easily away from the bone. Flambé with Cognac and serve with whipped potatoes.
Serves 4.

I once had an editor whom I invited to dinner six times and each time he refused. He didn't believe that a woman who was also a journalist could cook. But he accepted the seventh invitation and after that I had to teach his wife how to cook geese in this way. I like to say it's the result of blackmail.

3 blue geese (5 pounds each)
1 unpeeled orange, thinly sliced
12 juniper berries (optional)
1/4 pound butter
4 bay leaves
chopped leaves of 10 celery stalks

2 onions, cut up
2 cups apple juice
dash cinnamon
pinch each rosemary, tarragon and
    dried mint
Cognac

In a large ovenproof pan put the orange slices, juniper berries, butter, bay leaves, celery leaves, onions, then the geese. Sear the meat in a very hot (500°) oven for 10 minutes, then lower the heat to 350°. Baste geese liberally with the apple juice and sprinkle them with the cinnamon and herbs. Cook for 3-1/2 to 4 hours. Flambé with Cognac and serve. This recipe can be accompanied by baked apples, apple jelly or applesauce. Serves 6 to 8.

Bonne Femme is an emotional expression for us French-Canadians. It means not only the way of cooking, but the smile that goes with it, the clean white tablecloth and the tenderness of our grandmothers.

1/2 cup wild rice
pinch each thyme and savory
1-1/2 teaspoons powdered bay leaves
1 tablespoon each chopped parsley and
  chervil

2 cups water
1/4 cup long-grain white rice
butter

Soak the wild rice for 3 hours with the herbs in the water. Then bring it to a boil, cover tightly and cook over low heat for 50 minutes, adding the white rice only 15 minutes before the end of the cooking period. (If the rice seems to be sticking, add more water.) Mix in a few large lumps of butter before serving.
Serves 4.

SMALL GAME

Small game should be carefully cleaned and hung just as large game, although the hanging will not be as long and can be eliminated altogether if the animal is to be eaten immediately. A large hare will need as long as four days hanging in temperatures just above freezing.

Instructions on preparing small game before cooking are given on page 139.

Beavers that feed on birch taste better than those that feed on aspen. This recipe is the gracious contribution of Edgar Brochu, a former forester.

1 beaver tail (3 or 4 pounds)   4 large potatoes, peeled and sliced
4 large carrots, sliced   fines herbes
2 large onions, sliced

Skin the beaver tail. Cut the meat into 1-inch cubes. Boil for 1 to 1-1/2 hours together with the carrots, onions and potatoes, sprinkled with herbs.
Serves 4.

The Saint-Tropez restaurant in Montréal prepares beaver stew in the following, old-fashioned way, marinating the beaver for two weeks. I prefer to marinate it for a shorter period of three days.

1 beaver (5 to 6 pounds)	2 tablespoons fines herbes
red wine	1 tablespoon rosemary
olive oil	8 bay leaves
6 shallots, chopped	butter and olive oil

Cut up the beaver into 12 pieces. Place these in a large enamelware container and cover with a mixture of 1 part red wine to 2 parts olive oil. Mix in the shallots, fines herbes, rosemary and bay leaves. Marinate for 3 days to 2 weeks. Drain the meat and sauté it in an equal quantity of butter and olive oil. Strain the marinade and pour it over the meat. Cover and simmer over low heat for 3 to 4 hours.
Serves 10 to 12.

1 hare
1/4 pound butter
2 shallots, chopped
1 tablespoon flour
2 tablespoons tomato paste
1/2 cup red wine

1 garlic clove, crushed
pinch fines herbes
2 tablespoons chives
pepper
2 or 3 small tomatoes, cut up
1/4 pound fresh mushrooms, cut up

Cut the hare into 6 pieces and brown it in half of the butter in a baked-enamel pan. Add the shallots, the flour and the tomato paste and mix well. Then add the wine, an equal quantity of water, the garlic and the herbs. Cook over low heat for 1-1/2 to 2 hours. Half an hour before the end of the cooking time, fry in remaining butter the coarsely cut tomatoes and mushrooms and add them to the meat.
Serves 4.

1 hare
1/2 pound pork tenderloin
1/2 pound salt pork, blanched
1/2 pound veal (a slice of leg)
salt and pepper

pinch nutmeg
1/4 cup Cognac
2 large strips of pork fat
dash of thyme
3 bay leaves

Bone the hare, put aside the loins and sauté the liver in butter. Chop very finely the pork tenderloin, the salt pork and the veal. Remove the nerves from the legs of the hare before chopping the legs very finely too, together with the rest of the hare's meat, including the liver. Season with salt, pepper and nutmeg. Add the Cognac and mix all the meats together.

Line the bottom of a terrine with a strip of pork fat, then put in a layer of chopped meats and part of the hare loin on top of that. Repeat the operation with alternate layers of ground meat and loin until the terrine is filled. Sprinkle with thyme, then place a few bay leaves on top and cover with the other strip of pork fat. Place the terrine with its lid on in a pan of hot water in the oven and cook at 350° for 1-1/2 hours. Before taking it out of the oven make sure that the pâté is cooked by pricking it with a long needle. It should go in easily and the juice coming out should be clear. Remove from the oven, replace the lid by a plate or a bowl to press the meat down while it is cooling. If you wish to keep the pâté for a few days, remove the bay leaves and pour a small amount of melted lard over the top.

Hare (or rabbit) tastes a bit like chicken—the wild hare has dark meat, while the domestic version has light meat. This recipe reminds me of the most surrealistic experience I've ever had in the bush. It was seeing an Italian family hunting for hare, with the grandmother, the mother and the daughters walking along beating their casseroles to flush the game!

1 hare
4 tablespoons white bread crumbs
4 tablespoons grated Parmesan cheese
1 egg

salt and pepper
1/4 pound butter
1/2 cup tomato juice

Cut the hare into 6 pieces and flatten them out by pounding the meat gently. Have two soup plates ready, one in which you mix the bread crumbs and grated Parmesan, and the other in which you beat an egg with salt and pepper. Roll the pieces of hare in the Parmesan and crumbs, then in the beaten egg, then again in the Parmesan and crumbs. Fry in butter over medium heat for 45 minutes. Then add the tomato juice and cook for another hour over very low heat.
Serves 4.

1 hare (3 pounds)
butter
3 or 4 strips pork fat
salt and pepper
2 tablespoons chopped parsley

Stuffing:
2 cups mashed potatoes
1 small onion, finely chopped
5 pork sausages or 1/4 pound pork
  sausage meat

After washing the hare let it soak for 2 to 3 hours in salt water—allowing 2 tablespoons of salt to each quart of water. Dry it well and stuff it with the mashed potatoes mixed with the onion and pork sausages without their skins. Then brush the hare with a little butter, cover it with thin strips of pork fat and place it in a roasting pan. Season it with salt and pepper and parsley and roast it in a 400° oven for 30 minutes. Then lower the heat to 300° for the rest of the cooking time—another 1 to 1-1/2 hours. Baste from time to time with 1/4 cup butter melted in 1/2 cup boiling water.
Serves 2 or 3.

If your husband wants to prove how skillful a hunter he is to your oldest son, suggest that he catch a squirrel with a sling shot, dry the pelt and mount it. Then you will be able to cook this delicacy.

2 large squirrels
2 wide strips of pork fat
1 carrot, sliced
1 unpeeled orange, sliced
2 shallots, coarsely chopped
2 bay leaves

4 tablespoons fines herbes
1 tablespoon chives
1 cup white wine
juice of 3 oranges
vodka or gin (optional)

Carefully wrap the squirrels in strips of pork fat and put them in a roasting pan with the carrot, the orange slices, the chopped shallots, the herbs and the white wine. Roast in the oven at 350° for 1-1/2 hours. Half an hour after the beginning of the cooking, add the orange juice. Strain the sauce before serving. Flambé with vodka or gin if you wish. Serves 2.

This recipe is the gracious contribution of a friend who never even offered me a muskrat cap. Cook it for your husband as revenge, if you don't get your mink coat for Christmas.

1 muskrat (2 to 3 pounds)	pinch rosemary
red wine	4 bay leaves
olive oil	1/4 pound butter
3 shallots, chopped	1 12-ounce can black cherries
1 tablespoon fines herbes	1 tablespoon red currant jelly (optional)

Cut the muskrat into 4 large pieces and place them in a large bowl or enamelware pan. Cover the pieces with a mixture of 1 part wine to 2 parts olive oil and mix in the shallots, herbs, rosemary and bay leaves. Let marinate for 48 hours. Remove the meat and strain the marinade. Sauté the meat in butter, then add the strained marinade and cook over low heat for 1-1/2 to 2 hours. Half an hour before the end of the cooking time, add the cherries with their juice and the currant jelly.
Serves 2 or 3.

LARGE GAME

In the French language, we call meat from all large game venison—stag, roe deer, fallow deer and wild boar. In Québec it also includes Virginia deer, caribou and moose (the European deer does not exist in North America).

If cooks so often look down on venison, it is because hunters do such a bad job of butchering game. It is, therefore, absolutely essential to have the butchering done properly. The animal must be cooled quickly, thoroughly cleaned and carefully transported and preserved. The more care the hunter takes in the woods, the more good, tender, edible meat will make it to the kitchen.

The best cuts to use for steaks are (in order of preference) the chops, sirloin, sirloin tip, round and (in young deer only) the shoulder.

For roasts choose the sirloin first, then the ribs, rump, shoulder and the flank, spareribs, shank or neck. Make stews from the spareribs, brisket, neck and shoulder.

Instructions on preparing large game before cooking are given on page 138.

MARINATING GAME

The first principle in marinating meat is to use a good quality of dry wine (never, never sweet), the same wine that you will serve with the meal. Game can be marinated in seasoned water with vinegar added, but wine is so much better. You may also help tenderize the meat by inserting lardoons of salt pork in it before you marinate it. Remember that it is always dangerous to overmarinate meat, because you might kill its natural flavor.

SEASONING FOR LARGE GAME

Never, never put salt on meat before cooking it. Salt makes it tough. Besides, a very good cook never needs to put much salt in anything, if the other seasonings are properly balanced. Putting salt on everything shows a lack of imagination and self-confidence.

I want to make a note for your reflections. Why, during the hunting season, does the buck always allow one or two females to go ahead of him? Is he such an emancipated animal that he doesn't care? Or is he afraid?

4 to 6 deer chops   pinch of sugar
3 tablespoons butter   salt and pepper
finely chopped parsley   1/4 cup bouillon
1/4 teaspoon thyme   1 tablespoon wine vinegar
1 garlic clove, chopped   1/2 teaspoon flour
1 small bay leaf

Sauté the chops on both sides in 2 tablespoons of the butter over high heat in a heavy frying pan. Lower the heat and add the parsley, thyme, garlic, bay leaf, sugar and salt and pepper. Pour the bouillon over this and cook gently for 5 minutes. Remove the chops and place them on a warm serving dish. Stir in the frying pan the vinegar, the remaining tablespoon of butter and the flour. Keep stirring briskly and heat without letting the sauce boil. Strain the sauce before pouring it over the chops.
Serves 4 to 6.

The best pot to cook this in is a bean pot.

4 pounds ground deer meat	8 small onions
6 shallots, finely chopped	24 small new potatoes
6 parsley sprigs, chopped	8 medium carrots, cut up
2 tablespoons chopped chives	2 tablespoons olive oil
dash pepper	2-1/2 cups mixed vegetable juice
powdered bay leaves	

Mix together the ground deer meat, the finely chopped shallots, parsley, chives, pepper and bay leaves. Roll this mixture into 32 small meatballs. In a baked-enamel dish or a stoneware crock, put the onions, potatoes, carrots and olive oil. Place the meatballs on top and pour the vegetable juice over them. Bake covered, except for the last 25 minutes, in a 350° oven for 2 hours. Serve with garden peas.
Serves 8.

I like deer and I hate liver. The reality of those two feelings together makes me dream of the day when my understanding of the *yin* and *yang* principle will be integrated in my bones and liver.

1 deer liver	1 piece salt pork
6 parsley sprigs	salt and pepper
5 shallots	1 tablespoon olive oil

Cut the liver into thick slices. Chop together the parsley, shallots and salt pork. Sprinkle with salt and pepper. Put a good coating of this mixture on each slice of liver. Heat olive oil in a saucepan and cook liver gently uncovered over a low heat for 45 minutes. Serves 4.

Just a suggestion—a hunting club should get together to prepare these deer sausages and share them afterwards with their sportsmen friends. The advantage of this is that there is only one kitchen to clean up instead of four or five. And only one infuriated housewife instead of five. If you're lucky, you'll make 599 sausages because I believe you'll lose one in the preparation.

skins for approximately 600 sausages
25 pounds ground deer meat (flank, brisket, shank, neck, offals)
25 pounds ground pork (50 percent lean meat)
5 quarts ice water

1/2 cup salt
3-1/2 pounds unsalted soda crackers, crushed into crumbs, or bread crumbs
6 tablespoons white pepper
4 tablespoons nutmeg
1 tablespoon sage (optional)

Mix all the ingredients together well and stuff the sausage skins with them, or else shape into croquettes 1 inch thick. Cook as you would any sausage.

1 or 2 pounds deer or moose steaks
1 cup olive oil
1 pound fresh mushrooms, sliced
2 stalks celery, finely chopped
1 teaspoon oregano
1 red chili pepper, crushed

1 garlic clove, crushed
1 tomato, cut in 6 pieces
1 6-ounce can tomato paste
2 tablespoons grated Parmesan cheese
butter

To make the sauce, brown in olive oil the mushrooms, the celery, the oregano and chili pepper. Add the garlic, the cut-up tomato, the tomato paste and the grated cheese. Season to taste. Cook over a very low heat for at least 1 hour. Grill the steak or fry it in a very hot cast-iron pan with a small lump of butter. Be moderate when you pour the sauce over the steaks as it is very spicy; serve the remaining sauce on the side.
Serves 2 to 4.

In the antiquity of 10 years ago, when women were not emancipated, four girls and I were coming back from a hunting trip at Mont-Laurier. The game warden stopped us and, because he didn't believe that we had killed our own moose, like William Tell we had to prove to him that we were five sharpshooters. You can use this recipe equally well for a deer tenderloin.

1 moose tenderloin, cut in 4 pieces
2 cups olive oil
1 cup red wine
2 small onions, chopped
1 carrot, sliced
4 bay leaves

8 peppercorns
1 tablespoon chopped parsley
1/4 pound butter
1/4 cup strong black coffee
1/4 cup red wine or 2 tablespoons
    marinade

Let the meat marinate for a maximum of 4 hours in a mixture of the olive oil, wine, onions, carrots, bay leaves and peppercorns. Take it out, dry it, and cook it in some of the butter, as you would a small beef steak, to rare or medium according to taste. Place the steaks in a chafing dish to keep them warm. Melt the remaining butter over high heat until it begins to brown, then add the coffee and the red wine or 2 tablespoons of the marinade. Simmer slowly until the sauce turns a rich dark color and pour it over the steaks. Serve with sautéed potatoes.
Serves 4.

2 pounds ground moose meat
1 pound ground pork
1 pound fresh mushrooms, sliced
2 large garlic cloves, crushed
1 green pepper, chopped (optional)
1 tomato, chopped (optional)
1 to 2 stalks celery, chopped (optional)
4 to 6 tablespoons olive oil

bay leaves
1 or more red chili peppers, crushed
1 tablespoon fresh oregano
pinch paprika
coarsely ground black pepper
4 shallots, finely chopped
1 6-ounce can tomato paste
cooked spaghetti or macaroni

In a baked enamel pan gently sauté the mushrooms and garlic (with the green pepper, tomato and celery if you are using) in olive oil over very low heat until the mushrooms begin to brown. Add the herbs and spices. Meanwhile mix together the moose and pork meat with the shallots and add to the nicely browned mushrooms. Continue cooking at low temperature until the juice is brown. Add the tomato paste and some olive oil if the sauce is too thick. Cover the pan and simmer for 2 hours, stirring frequently to keep the sauce from burning or sticking to the bottom of the pan. Serve over spaghetti or macaroni.
Serves 4.

2 pounds moose shoulder meat
paprika
coarsely ground black pepper
1/4 pound butter
1 small onion, minced
1 tablespoon fines herbes

2 to 3 cups beef stock
4 tablespoons flour
1 cup red wine
1 pound fresh mushrooms, sliced
butter

Cut the meat into 1-1/2 inch cubes and sprinkle it with paprika and pepper. Brown it in butter with the onion. Add the herbs. Cover the meat with the beef stock and simmer covered over a low heat for 1-1/2 to 2 hours. Halfway through the cooking add the flour mixed with the red wine. Half an hour before serving, sauté the mushrooms in butter and add.
Serves 6.

1 pound ground fillet of moose
4 crushed bay leaves
coarsely ground black pepper
pinch paprika
fines herbes
1 tablespoon chives
1 tablespoon finely chopped parsley

1 large stalk celery, finely chopped
2 shallots, finely chopped
8 slices bacon
1/4 pound butter
1/4 cup red wine
1 tablespoon coffee (optional)

Sprinkle the ground moose meat with the spices and herbs and mix with the celery and shallots. Divide the meat into 4 parts and shape it into 4 large patties 1-1/4 inches thick. Wrap 2 slices of bacon around each patty and secure them with toothpicks. Sauté the meat patties in half the butter at high temperature, then lower the heat and continue cooking to rare or medium according to taste. Remove patties from skillet and make a sauce with remaining butter and the red wine. You may wish to add 1 tablespoon of coffee. This is excellent when served with sautéed mushrooms.
Serves 4.

1 large cabbage
2 ounces wild rice
1-1/3 cups water
1-1/2 pounds ground moose meat
1/2 pound ground pork
1 red chili pepper, crushed

1 teaspoon oregano
dash cayenne
pinch tarragon
1/4 pound butter
2 cups tomato juice

Blanch the cabbage. Soak the wild rice and boil it for 50 minutes. Mix together the ground moose and pork meat with herbs and spices. Then add the cooked rice. Place a dab of this mixture on each cabbage leaf, roll up and secure the rolls with toothpicks. Place them in a well-buttered baking dish and cover them with the tomato juice. Bake in the oven at 325° for 1-1/2 hours and serve.
Serves 6 to 8.

Fries are technically testicles, but it's so much nicer to call them "amourettes." In the Western United States they are known as Rocky Mountain oysters, I've been told. This recipe was given to me by the National Meat Institute in Montreal.

2 moose fries
flour, salt and pepper
butter

Remove the outer skin of the fries and slice them thinly. Dredge the slices lightly with flour seasoned with salt and pepper. Fry in butter at medium heat for 8 to 10 minutes. The meat must be well cooked.
Serves 2.

Unfortunately I have never had a chance to prepare a cut of bear meat myself. However, I have had the pleasure of tasting a roast leg of bear, and I am glad to pass on the recipe.

1 leg of bear (10 pounds)
olive oil
red wine
2 carrots, cut up
2 onions, cut up
2 celery stalks, including leaves, cut up
6 to 8 cups beef stock

Pepper Sauce:
2 shallots, chopped
2 tablespoons butter
10 peppercorns, freshly ground
2 tablespoons flour
1 cup red wine
salt
1 bay leaf
pinch each tarragon and chervil

Marinate the leg for 12 hours in olive oil and red wine to cover (2 parts olive oil to 1 part red wine) with the carrots, onions and celery. Drain the meat well and brown it on all sides. Discard the surplus fat, add the beef stock and put in the oven at 450° for the first half hour. Then turn down the heat to 350° for the rest of the cooking time which should be from 1 to 1-1/2 hours more. This roast should be eaten rare, carved into slices 1 inch thick, and served with the following pepper sauce.

To make the pepper sauce, brown the chopped shallots in butter in a heavy saucepan. Sprinkle with a generous amount of black pepper and add the flour, the drippings from the roast, the wine, a little salt, the bay leaf, tarragon and chervil. Let the sauce simmer until it is nice and brown. If it gets too thick add a little consommé, and if you find it too strong, sweeten it with some cream.

I name this recipe after Grandmother because I have added coffee to the sauce as she used to do. Adding coffee or tea to a meat sauce was a secret of many French-Canadian cooks of the last century, but you don't find it used very often in our cooking today.

3 pounds caribou meat   1 garlic clove, slivered
olive oil   flour
red wine   dry mustard
1 onion, cut up   butter
1 carrot, cut up   coarsely ground black pepper
4 bay leaves   ground bay leaves
8 black peppercorns

Let your piece of meat marinate for 3 to 6 hours according to taste in a mixture of olive oil and red wine, together with the onion, carrot, bay leaves and black peppercorns. Turn the meat over regularly so that it soaks up the marinade. Dry it carefully before cooking and insert the garlic slivers in slits in the meat. Dredge the meat lightly with flour and dry mustard, then garnish it with generous lumps of butter and sprinkle it with ground pepper and bay. Roast in the oven at 500° for 30 to 35 minutes. The meat should be quite rare in the middle. Serve with the following sauce.
Serves 6.

WINE SAUCE

1 small onion, chopped
butter
flour
1-1/2 cups of marinade from caribou
2 tablespoons of instant coffee or

1/4 cup strong black coffee, preferably
   Turkish
ground black peppercorns
ground bay leaves

Brown the onion in a generous lump of butter. Stir in a little flour and add the marinade, then the coffee and spices. Simmer for 10 to 12 minutes.

PIQUANT VERCHÈRES SAUCE FOR ROASTS

I call this sauce "Verchères," because I created the recipe when I was living in Verchères. It is not only delicious with game roasts, but with beef and lamb as well. Don't be afraid to use the entire head or bulb of garlic; it's the secret of the sauce.

1 entire head of garlic cloves
3/4 cup olive oil
3/4 cup mixed vegetable juice
1 6-ounce can tomato paste
1 tablespoon chopped parsley

1 teaspoon fines herbes
1/2 teaspoon Tabasco sauce
1 celery stalk, very thinly sliced
1 anise-flavored cornichon pickle, chopped
1/4 cup juice from pickles

Peel and crush the garlic cloves, adding the residue from the garlic inside the press to the crushed garlic. Combine this with all other ingredients and refrigerate until used. The sauce will keep for several weeks in the refrigerator.

PREPARING FISH AND GAME

If you wish to begin by scaling your fish, hold it firmly by the tail and scrape toward the head with a dull knife or scaler held at a 45 degree angle. If you do this under running water, you will avoid scattering the scales.

Next comes cleaning. Slit the skin from vent to gills and lift out the viscera; then remove the blood line against the backbone and rinse the inside of the fish thoroughly under running water. If you wish to remove the head, cut across the base of the gills and snap the backbone by bending it over the edge of the cutting board. The fins can be removed by cutting a slit along either side and pulling the fin sharply toward the head. This will lift out the root bones as well.

To fillet a fish, cut through the skin and flesh along the center of the back as far as the backbone from tail to just below the head. Then, holding the knife flat along the flesh, and starting at the head, cut the flesh on that side away from the bones. Remove the fillet. Turn the fish over and repeat. To skin a fillet, place it skin side down and cut the flesh away from skin which you hold in one hand. Slant the knife blade toward the skin so that no flesh is wasted.

To bone a fish, continue the slit from vent to tail. Then hold the fish firmly in one hand and insert the tip of the knife into the flesh close to the backbone. Cut the flesh from the backbone and ribs, staying as close to the bone as possible to avoid waste. Turn the fish over and cut the flesh away from the other side of the bones. Then loosen the backbone and discard it, or use it for making court bouillon.

Cooking fish requires a little care and attention because it is easy to overcook. In general, all fish is done when it flakes easily if a fork is inserted in the flesh and lifted slightly, and when the flesh is no longer transparent. When cooking fish with white flesh, always sprinkle it first with lemon juice to preserve the whiteness.

LARGE GAME

No amount of printed advice can be as valuable as the assistance of an experienced hunter when it comes to butchering large game, but if you do plan to go out on your own, the following advice should give you the general idea. The animal must first be bled by cutting the jugular vein at the base of the neck. The next step is to gut the carcass by slitting the skin from the breastbone to the vent, taking great care not to cut the intestines in order to avoid tainting the meat. Roll the skin back, taking care to keep loose hairs out of the meat. Carefully remove the internal organs after tying off the bladder and intestines before cutting them away. Wipe the internal cavity and, to make sure enough air gets in to quickly cool the flesh, use a stick to hold the flanks apart.

The meat should be transported carefully to avoid bruising, and should be wrapped in cheesecloth or other porous material (if wrapping is necessary), not plastic.

An animal which has been killed on the spot, without a chase, will always be more tender and this information should always be passed on to the cook. The length of time required for hanging varies with the age of the animal and the temperature, although the temperature should never be over 50°F. A male deer should hang unskinned for 10 to 15 days at 32°F to 34°F, or for seven days at 40°F. The skin should be left on to prevent the meat from drying out.

The best cuts to use for steaks are (in order of preference) the chops, sirloin, sirloin tip, round and (in young deer only) the shoulder.

For roasts choose the sirloin first, then the ribs, rump, shoulder and the flank, spareribs, shank or neck. Make stews from the spareribs, brisket, neck and shoulder.

If you would prefer having someone else look after the butchering (your local butcher, for example) make sure you consult him before going on your hunting trip, as there may still be special instructions and precautions for you to follow.

SMALL GAME

Skin small animals before cleaning by cutting the skin from around the back legs and pulling it off over the head which is then cut off. This is only one of several methods, but it is a useful all-purpose one for almost any type of small game.

WILDFOWL

First pluck out the larger feathers by hand, then pull out the pin feathers with tweezers. After that, remove the remaining down or fuzz by brushing the bird with a little paraffin melted in water—the feathers will pull out when it is peeled off—or by singeing over an open flame. To draw the bird, cut around the vent and remove the entrails, saving the giblets—heart, liver and gizzard. Take care when cleaning waterfowl to remove the two small oil glands, the size of a dry bean, which are situated at the back of the tail (pope's nose) and which provide the lubricant for the feathers so the bird can float. If you don't remove these the bird will taste like fish.

INDEX

FRANCINE DUFRESNE: LÉOPOLDINE

What is behind Léopoldine's name?
Another nickname: Dale-Galopping-Gloutnez-Doctor-Spock.
Behind all of these?
A French-Canadian journalist and writer, Francine Dufresne.

Francine was born in Montréal in the early forties. At fifteen she was a cashier in a grocery store, then a waitress specializing in the cooking of chicken salad at the Université de Montréal. She made her true debut at sixteen on radio. During the following 10 years she worked as a journalist in Montréal. She says of her career, "I made them (the Montréal newspapers) all."

One of the first women to be a member of the Outdoor Writers of Canada, Francine quickly became a real lover of the outdoors and an expert skeet-shooter and migratory-bird hunter. She also published two books on the cooking of fish and game and this book is a translation of the second of these. During the next three years she worked as public relations officer for the wife of the Premier of Québec, edited a woman's magazine and wrote a column for a weekly newspaper. She continued to write for radio and television as well as host shows for both *Radio Canada* and *Radio Québec.* To date she has also written three autobiographical novels which are best-sellers in French Canada: *A Woman In Freedom, Goddamn Solitude,* and the most recent, *God, That Clown.* One of her most recent projects has been a one-hour film made in Paris on music.

Francine Dufresne is a woman in love with the creative awareness in even the smallest life experience, and in order to feel alive she believes in constantly changing her approach to things. Never to cook the same way twice; never to make love the same way twice; never to repeat herself, never even to hear a piece of music twice with the same ears. Her main precept is that creativity in all things stems from the love of the task: "And I didn't learn that at school, but from loving people."